Revival, Revolution, and Religion in Early Virginia

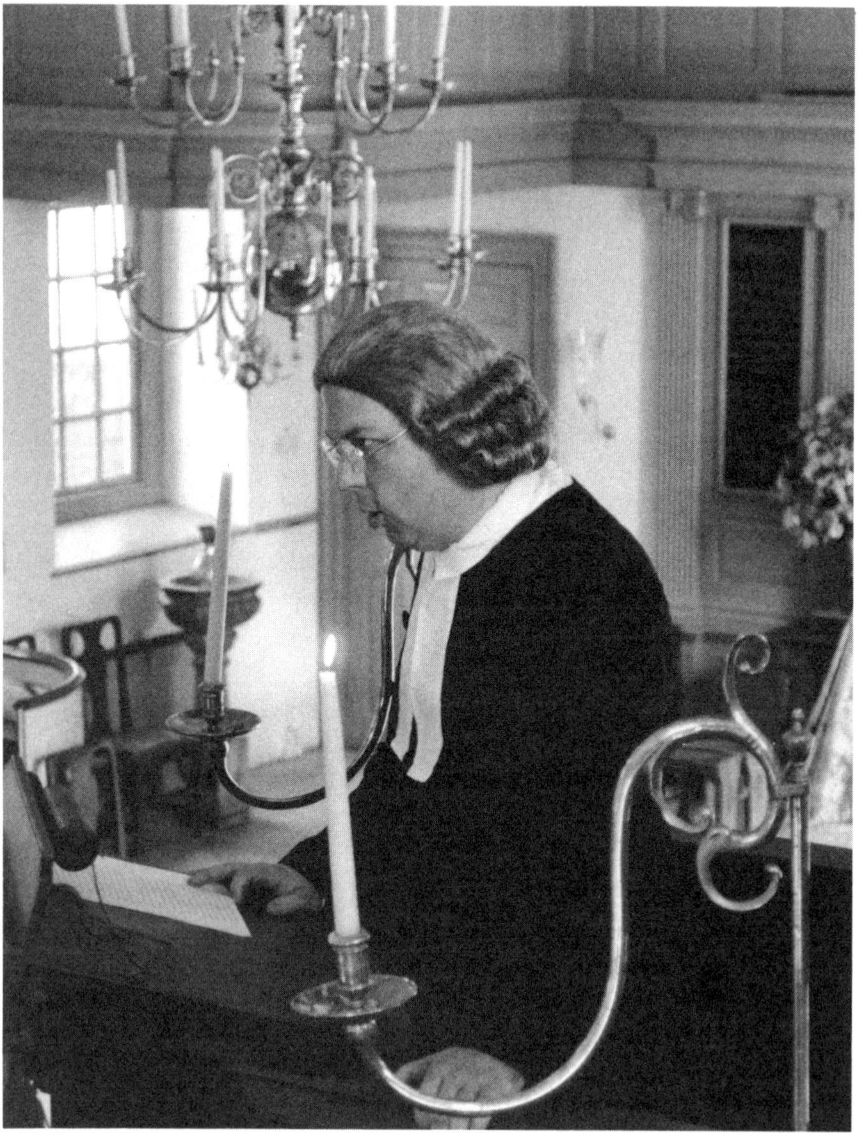

An interpreter portrays the Reverend Samuel Henley preaching at Bruton Parish Church in Williamsburg.

The Foundations of America

Revival, Revolution, and Religion in Early Virginia

By Edwin S. Gaustad

The Colonial Williamsburg Foundation
Williamsburg, Virginia

Printed in the United States of America

ISBN 0-87935-091-1

Cover, clockwise from lower left: An itinerant preacher, an Anglican minister, and an African-American preacher are depicted by interpreters at Colonial Williamsburg.

Revival, Revolution, and Religion in Early Virginia

"Men have traveled, as they have lived," Sir Walter Raleigh wrote in the sixteenth century, "for religion, for wealth, for knowledge, for pleasure, for power and the overthrow of rivals." Raleigh neatly summarized the mixture of motives that characterized the European exploration and settlement of the New World from the time of Christopher Columbus on. One notes, however, the motive that he placed first: religion. Whether considering the exploits of the Spanish, the French, or the English, religion—the proclamation of the Christian gospel and its dispersion across hitherto unknown lands—is much in evidence as these nations explored and as they planted settlements.

By 1600, Spain had already dispatched missionaries and soldiers into much of South and Central America as well as into portions of North America. Soon after 1600, France began establishing forts along the Saint Lawrence River, founding Quebec about the same time that the English founded Jamestown, Virginia. Jesuit missionaries moving up the Saint Lawrence River penetrated the interior of the North American continent, living with Indian tribes around the Great Lakes and encouraging the exploration of the headwaters of the Mississippi River. For the thirteen colonies that were to become the United States, however, England was the European power of greatest import. During the reign of Queen Elizabeth I (1558–1603), serious efforts at colonization got underway. When England's first permanent colony was planted along the shores of the James River, the whole area was named Virginia in honor of the "Virgin Queen."

The Anglican Establishment

In the sixteenth and seventeenth centuries, European nations all had official or national churches, that is, churches le-

John Smith's map of Virginia.

gally protected and supported by the government. Such churches, intimately identified with all of life, typically took charge of all education, supervised public and private morality, distributed charity to the poor, cared for orphans, the aged, and the ill, and frequently exercised great influence in the making and enforcing of laws. Such national churches, in other words, had an influence far beyond that which twentieth-century Americans observe in their communities. The notion that church, state, and society should somehow be "separate" was not only unwelcome in sixteenth-century Europe; the very idea was virtually impossible to comprehend. To the extent that it could be comprehended, it was widely denounced as the greatest folly, the equivalent of treason, and the end of any stable social order.

In both Spain and France the national church was Roman Catholic; in England it was Protestant, or, more precisely, Anglican. The Church of England (known today as the Episcopal church) followed England's flag wherever it was unfurled in the New World, just as the Roman Catholic church accompanied the explorations and settlements of Spain and France in the Western Hemisphere. Following their arrival in Virginia in 1607, English settlers intended that their colony faithfully reflect religious life and belief as cherished by their countrymen and women in the Old World. Each new town, settlers assumed, would soon look like the small English village with its prominent parish church and its busy minister supervising all the educational and charitable activities to be found there. This pattern never developed as expected, for the early settlers created a life that centered on plantations more than in villages. Families and their laborers were widely scattered along the banks of the broad rivers, so that when the time came to build churches, they stood not at the center of town life but in the sparsely populated countryside. Religion thus being more at the edge of life than at its very center created problems, not the least of which were the long distances involved in even getting to a church. As one traveler noted in 1740, both Virginia and Maryland suffered from "irreligion" since "people living at a distance from the church are apt to make every little thing serve as an excuse to keep them from public worship."

Williamsburg, the colonial capital of Virginia through most of the eighteenth century, was a modest exception to the predominantly rural character of the colony. With the erection of the college buildings in the early 1700s and the later enlargement of Bruton Parish Church along with the impressive governmental buildings—notably the Capitol and the Governor's Palace, the town seemed well on its way to becoming a real colonial city. But a single town could not alter the overwhelmingly rural character of the colony. And, Williamsburg itself reverted to its earlier status of a country village when the capital moved west to Richmond in 1780.

Besides a lack of urban centers, another difficulty facing the Church of England was that Virginia never had a bishop of its own during the colonial era. In England, bishops were indispensable in the life of the church; only they could perform the sacrament of confirmation; only they could ordain new priests for the church's ministry. Bishops sat in the House of Lords in Britain's Parliament. Bishops presided over ecclesiastical courts to enforce the discipline and doctrine of the church. Bishops

"An Interview between Sir Edmund Andros and James Blair" by Howard Pyle appeared in Harper's Monthly Magazine *for April 1901. Courtesy, Virginia State Library and Archives.*

advised the highest officials (even the kings and queens) on all matters pertaining to the welfare and advancement of England. Yet, for reasons to be explained later, no bishops ever resided in colonial Virginia. This absence of direct ecclesiastical supervision sharply limited the effectiveness of the official church in this part of the New World. Virginia did enjoy the presence of a "commissary" representing the bishop of London who, more by accident than design, had overall responsibility for ecclesiastical affairs in the colonies. The royal governor, moreover, sought to encourage the stability and enlargement of the Church of England in Virginia. At many points in the eighteenth century, however, the two most powerful men in the colony—the commissary and the governor—worked against each other rather than being joined in a cordial and productive alliance.

Thus, although Virginia granted legal protection and support to its official church (just as England did back home), the changed conditions of geography, the lack of bishops, and the struggle just to survive in a wilderness made the progress of Anglicanism in the new colony both difficult and slow. Nonetheless, by the end of the seventeenth century, the Church of England was stronger in Virginia than it was anywhere else in North America. By 1750 Virginia and Maryland together had as many Anglican churches within their borders as did all the rest of the thirteen colonies put together. Of course, some of the British colonies had a much later start than did Virginia or Maryland (for example, the Carolinas and Georgia), while others deliberately sought an alternative to England's national church (for example, Puritan Massachusetts and Quaker Pennsylvania).

By the middle of the eighteenth century, therefore, one might have assumed that the Church of England was so firmly established in Virginia as to remain forever the dominant religious institution of the area. Challenges to the religious monopoly in Virginia, however, had already begun. As early as the 1640s, some Puritans from Massachusetts settled in Nansemond County, growing before the end of the decade to a congregation of more than one hundred souls. Virginia governor William Berkeley, however, denounced this challenge to the colony's official religion and forced the Puritans to flee to Maryland. Quakers (or the Society of Friends) came to America soon after their founding in England in 1651, searching for safe havens up and down the Atlantic coast. In the 1660s they tried their luck in Virginia, but restrictive laws made the colony inhospitable to them—though not quite as inhospitable as Massachusetts, where four Quakers were hanged.

In 1689 England, after decades of its own religious turbulence, adopted an Act of Toleration. Theoretically, this act applied to England's colonies with equal force, though legal toleration was honored unevenly in the several colonies. And toleration, it should also be noted, was not the equivalent of religious freedom. The Toleration Act still allowed for a national church with special privileges and powers, but the law forbade the persecuting and punishing (and hanging) of those who held to other religious opinions.

Colonial Virginia slowly began to extend some measure of toleration to non-Anglicans. In 1713, for example, some German refugees (Church of the Brethren) found safety in Virginia from European persecution, just as two decades earlier some French Protestants (Huguenots) had escaped to the security of the Carolinas and Virginia. And by the middle of the eighteenth century, colonial Virginia no longer appeared to be a special Anglican "preserve," protected all around from dissenters and nonconformists—that is, from persons who adhered to neither the theology nor the liturgy of the Church of England. But the struggle for acceptance in Virginia, and the further struggle from mere toleration to full freedom, was both bitter and dramatic. The purpose of this essay is to explain those events that in only one half-century (from about 1750 to about 1800) greatly altered the religious landscape of early Virginia and powerfully prepared a whole nation for new approaches in relating religion to the civil and social order.

The Great Awakening

In the 1740s and 1750s, a religious revival swept across the American colonies from southernmost Georgia to northernmost New Hampshire. This period of religious excitement, later called the Great Awakening, had its parallel on the European continent among the pietists (for example, the Moravians of Bohemia) and in England (most conspicuously the Methodists, who first arose within the Church of England, but then broke away from it).

Everywhere the Awakening led many people to a far more serious and personal interest in religion than they had ever had before. Worship in the Church of England, in accordance with the Book of Common Prayer, tended to be formal, restrained, and intellectual. Worship inspired by the Awakening, on the other hand, tended to be spontaneous, joyful, and emotional. As a consequence, the Awakening moved more outside the Anglican church or even in opposition to it, adding greatly to the numbers of dissenters from the official religion. As a further consequence, the Awakening had more success in reaching Virginia's black population than the Anglican church had achieved in a century.

Slavery grew slowly in the early years of Virginia's settlement, but by the end of the seventeenth century it had become the chief labor source for the colony's plantations. And while there is historically no necessary connection between slavery and race (in the Roman Empire, Greeks were often the slaves), in Virginia and elsewhere in colonial America the connection came to be almost an identity: slaves were black, and blacks (with a few exceptions) were slaves. The Anglican emphasis on book-based liturgy and elaborate instruction had little in common with the African religious heritage of the newly arrived blacks. Masters, moreover, were often reluctant to allow slaves time away from their labors to receive the indoctri-

George Whitefield.

nation deemed necessary. Further, until Virginia laws clarified the matter, many argued that making a slave a Christian might automatically emancipate him or her. Even when lawmakers ruled that religious conversion did not bring civil liberty, masters gave slight encouragement to their slaves' religious interests.

An Anglican missionary organization formed in 1701, the Society for the Propagation of the Gospel, instructed its missionaries to "use their best endeavors, at proper times to instruct the Negroes." But in 1730 the society secretary confessed his deep disappointment that little had been accomplished among the blacks. The masters, he reported, had not been helpful at all. "Some," he added in dismay, "have been so weak as to argue that Negroes have no souls; others, that they grew worse by being taught and made Christians. I would not mention these if they were not popular arguments now, because they have no foundation in reason or truth."

The Awakening, by stressing one's personal experience, one's joyful acceptance of a gospel of redemption and cleansing, one's immediate understanding of the major religious truths, appealed to blacks and whites alike who had not found the liturgical formalism of the Church of England spiritually nourishing. To such hungry souls, the fresh and exciting oratory of young George Whitefield, recently arrived from England, seemed to have been sent from heaven. Visiting Williamsburg and other Virginia communities in 1739, the twenty-five-year-old Whitefield preached in Anglican churches if they would have him, in open fields if they would not. Drawing eager and fascinated crowds wherever he went, the dramatic orator seemed to make the Christian religion open to all equally: male or female, rich or poor, black or white, slave or free. (See Appendix A.) "Whosoever will, may come." So new, so startling did this message appear that many thought it called for new messengers (not the formal and official clergy of the Church of England), and perhaps for new churches as well. It was a time to start over in Virginia, with a fresh understanding of what being a Christian meant and with a reawakened zeal for the truths of religion.

The Presbyterians and Samuel Davies

The Great Awakening, like revivalism generally, did not emphasize loyalty to a specific denomination. It emphasized, rather, the personal conversion, the new birth, the gospel not of society but of salvation. If the Church of England was too closely tied to kings and parliaments, to bishops and books, then perhaps one could better express the newly adopted faith in some other religious institution.

Samuel Davies, more than any other single clergyman, made Presbyterianism appear an attractive alternative to the Church of England. Coming to Hanover County from Delaware in 1747, Davies determined within a year to make Virginia his permanent home. Like Whitefield, he won many hearers through his powerful preaching. And like Whitefield, he did not think that the Church of England had, or should have, any monopoly on true Christianity. He protested against all those Virginia laws that set one kind of church, and one kind of clergyman, on a higher legal plane than another. Despite England's Act of

Samuel Davies.
Courtesy, Princeton University.

Toleration, now more than half a century old, Davies encountered great difficulty in receiving permission to preach whenever and wherever he wished. For Davies, in addition to being a Presbyterian, was an itinerant—that is, he was a traveling preacher, not a preacher settled in a single community. The Awakening had introduced this novel idea too: that clergy need not be limited to a single parish, but could carry the gospel wherever they felt called by God to go.

Virginia was unaccustomed to this very non-Anglican approach to religion: preaching anywhere one could find or draw a crowd, creating a church wherever one could manage to do so, following the dictates of the Holy Spirit instead of the laws of Parliament. When itinerants first began invading Virginia in the 1740s (Davies among them), Governor William Gooch argued that these men were all "false teachers" who professed "themselves ministers under the pretended influence of new light, extraordinary impulse, and such like fanatical and enthusiastical knowledge." Davies insisted that, under the provision of the Act of Toleration, he had a right to preach. Virginia authorities insisted that, if he were given that right, it applied only to a single locality and was definitely not a license to wander all over the place as the mood struck him. The Reverend William Dawson, Virginia's leading Anglican minister and representative of the bishop of London, declared in 1752, "I think it high time for the Government to interpose, to give immodesty a check and to restrain their teachers [ministers] within the bounds of a parish." If, Dawson added, such ministers were not willing to abide by Anglican rules, so much the better. Then people would continue to attend the Church of England "whither they contentedly would have gone, if Mr. Davies had never come among them."

Such sentiments left Samuel Davies undaunted. He would not back away from what he perceived to be not only his civil liberty but also his religious duty. "I am not fond . . . of disseminating sedition and schism," he wrote to Dawson; "I have no ambition to Presbyterianize the colony." But, Davies added, he did have "a sincere zeal" to preach the universal truths of Christianity, the "grand essentials of our holy Religion," and to make "sincere practical Christians" of as many souls anywhere in Virginia as might attend to his message. By the time that Samuel Davies left Virginia in 1759 to accept the presidency of the College of New Jersey (later Princeton), he and other dissenters had won a measure of toleration in Virginia, but not yet that full freedom that would follow only upon a revolution.

Like Whitefield, Davies also concerned himself with the colony's blacks, among whom Anglicanism had proved so ineffective. Blacks had no separate churches at this time but were relegated to the margins of white churches, but worshiping in the same buildings and generally at the same time as their masters. The crowds that gathered to hear a Whitefield or a Davies in the meadows or along the roads were likewise composed of both black and white listeners. But blacks did have some distinctive needs, Davies recognized, one of which was surely more education. If the inability to read or write stood in the way of their full participation in the Christian religion, then, Davies reasoned, they must be taught these skills. He requested from England more books for the "poor neglected Negroe Slaves . . . [who] are so far from having money to purchase books that they themselves are the property of others."

The books that proved most popular among African-Americans were those containing the Psalms and hymns. Blacks flocked to Davies's own home for instruction but remained long after just to sing. "Sundry of them have lodged all night in my kitchen," Davies reported, "and sometimes, when I have awaked about two or three a-clock in the morning, a torrent of sacred harmony poured into my chamber, and carried my mind away to Heaven." Davies did not attack the institution of slavery as such, but he did labor to make it more humane. In 1758 he published a small book entitled *The Duty of Christians.* Addressing himself especially to the masters, Davies reminded them that Christ died for all and that no man could be a good Christian if he neglected the spiritual welfare of those placed under his care. Masters must never "act as though immortality were not a common privilege" of slave and free alike.

The Methodists and Devereux Jarratt

Others in the 1740s and 1750s proclaimed in Virginia the message of new birth and the call for a new spirit. Virginia's Anglicans resented the Methodist movement even more than the Presbyterian one, for Methodism arose within the established church's own bosom. In England the brothers John and Charles Wesley proposed a more "methodical" Christian life within the Anglican church. They emphasized regular reading of the Bible, offering devotions, prayers, and stated meeting times for telling others of the Christian experience. To promote this more earnest degree of spiritual commitment, the Wesleys organized small societies within the Church of England, their idea being to reform the whole national church little by little. Gradually, however, these Methodist societies began to take on a life of their own; soon they were seen not as gentle instruments of reform but as rude threats to the unity and harmony of England's established church. In the 1740s the bishop of London wrote to his Anglican clergy in Virginia to warn them against the arrival of Methodist itinerants; he also sent hastily written tracts "as an antidote against the spreading of that sect." The Methodists were not simply more zealous Christians, but unrestrained and unpredictable fanatics, the bishop wrote; "there is no reasoning with people who have got it into their heads that they think and act under the immediate guidance of the Spirit."

Most Anglican clergy in Virginia were prepared to agree with the bishop of London. One exception was Devereux Jarratt of Dinwiddie County who had been converted under the influence of the Great Awakening. An Anglican revivalist himself, Jarratt in the 1770s openly cooperated with the Methodists, thereby gaining the enmity of many of his fellow Anglicans. They called him, he wrote, "an enthusiast, fanatic, visionary, dissenter, Presbyterian madman and what not." Whatever the epithets thrown at Jarratt, he turned them aside to emphasize—as Whitefield and Davies had done—the personal side of religion, the enormous burden of sin, and the even greater supernatural release from that burden that none could bear alone.

By 1774 the Methodists had established their first "circuit" in Virginia: the regular visitation route for Methodism's itinerants, better known as circuit riders. While Jarratt remained an Anglican, he joined with well-known Methodist preachers in traveling far from his own parish in Bath to spread this new religion that valued experience above tradition and spirit above form. In 1784, Methodism finally made the break with Anglicanism official by organizing itself (in Baltimore) into a separate denomination. By that time, it was clear that the efforts of the bishop of London as well as of Virginia authorities forty years earlier had failed; "the spreading of that sect" had continued unabated, as Anglicanism withdrew more and more from the evangelical awakening.

An itinerant preacher is portrayed by an interpreter at Colonial Williamsburg.

The Baptists and John Leland

Throughout America, the mid-eighteenth century was a time of great growth for the Baptists. A small denomination earlier, and not a vigorously expanding one, this group was singularly invigorated by the Great Awakening. Particularly in New England, which also had its official religion of Congregationalism (or Puritanism), the widespread revival encouraged many people to leave the established church and create churches more congenial to traveling ministers and reborn members. Many who left the Congregational fold became Baptists, and many of these migrated southward, taking hold with special strength in the Carolinas and Virginia. One Anglican observer was particularly distressed by what he found in North Carolina in the early 1760s: "[T]hese Baptists have taken such deep Root there that it will require long Time and Pains to grub up their Layers." So also in Virginia, where sixty-seven new Baptist churches sprang into existence in the single decade of the 1770s. Much of this growth came from nearby North Carolina, but much also from the tireless labors of another traveling preacher, John Leland.

In 1776 John Leland left Massachusetts for Virginia, remaining there for fifteen years to persuade on behalf of his own church and to protest the privileges of yet another officially established church. Like those evangelicals whom we have already discussed, Leland dismissed religion that depended upon

John Leland.
Courtesy, The Berkshire Museum.

legal favors and tax assessors for its survival. Such religion, he charged, was not only tempted to fine and whip and jail those that differed with it, but it was also in danger of becoming internally corrupt itself. When a state pays for a church, he reasoned, then a state begins to think that it *is* a church. Religion then becomes a matter of official policy, and doctrine a question for Parliament to decide. All Protestants rejected the Pope in Rome, Leland noted, but many Protestants merely substituted their own king or council or legislature for the papal authority. Such civil authorities thought they had the right to determine what men and women should believe, how they should worship, whom they should hear, and so on. All of this made a mockery of religion and treated God as a kind of political hack. How have civil authorities behaved when they have taken over the churches, Leland asked. He answered, "One year make a law, and the next alter, repeal or undo it. Does God annually, or periodically change? If not, these law makers change; and are changeable men competent to direct men how to worship an unchangeable God?"

Like Samuel Davies, Leland found the condition of African-Americans in Virginia a matter of particular concern. "The whole scene of slavery," Leland wrote in 1790, "is pregnant with enormous evils. On the master's side, pride, haughtiness, domination, cruelty, deceit and intolerance; and on the side of the slave, ignorance, servility, fraud, perfidy and despair." With so many obvious evils attending the institution of slavery, the obvious question was, Why not do away with it? "Would to Heaven this were done!" Leland responded. Yet the Baptist itinerant recognized, as even his hero Thomas Jefferson did, that the practical difficulties were enormous: How could one dispose of or confiscate so much private property—for slaves were property? How could one provide for so many newly emancipated but unemployed people—for slaves were also persons? Leland estimated the value of all slaves in Virginia in 1790 to be more than eight million British pounds, "infinitely beyond what the commonwealth could pay to the holders of slaves for their ransom." And yet, Leland concluded, "It is the peculiarity of God to bring light out of darkness, good out of evil, order out of confusion." Leland found comfort in the fact that so many blacks turned to Christianity in general, and to the Baptists in particular. That was one ground for hope, as was the assurance, said Leland, that "common justice" would one day prevail for all Virginians, black or white, each claiming his or her own "birth-right blessing—*freedom*."

The Crisis Concerning Bishops

During the fifteen years that John Leland was in Virginia, from 1776 to 1791, much happened there as well as throughout all the colonies—colonies on their way to becoming states. Before the nation declared its independence and undertook its long and costly revolution, the Anglican church desperately tried to strengthen its own deteriorating position in Virginia and elsewhere by encouraging the arrival of bishops. Ironically, this effort convinced many Americans that a revolution was the only means of avoiding the presence of imperious and repressive spiritual overlords from England.

Before the 1689 Act of Toleration, bishops in England had earned the reputation of persecutors and powerful oppressors. They had driven the Baptists to Holland early in the seventeenth century; in the 1630s they had forced the Puritans to escape to a New England; in the 1660s, under a restored monarchy, they had turned against the Quakers and Presbyterians. Now, a century later, was there any reason to believe that English bishops would prove more benevolent and tolerant in the New World than they had in the Old? In Virginia the rapidly growing numbers of Presbyterians, Methodists, and Baptists saw Anglican bishops as a clear threat to the toleration for which they had struggled, year by year, county by county.

Anglicans, on the other hand, especially the clergy among them, believed that those who talked most of tolerance were themselves being unreasonably intolerant in their loud opposition to any and all bishops. The Church of England depended on the presence of bishops for its full and proper status as a denomination. If Virginia's Anglicans could eventually learn to tolerate a zealot like Davies, a fanatic like Jarratt, a vagabond like Leland, why could not these dissenters learn to accept a bishop?

Long before dissent became a major factor in the religious history of Virginia, Anglicans argued that a bishop in the colony would "make Hell tremble and settle the Church of England in these parts forever." When by the 1760s no bishop had yet come and dissent was growing ever stronger, the patience of Anglicans grew short and their rhetoric sharp. But the 1760s were also the years of the Stamp Act, the Townshend Acts, colonial resolves, and protests. The decade ended with the shedding of blood in front of the Boston customhouse in 1770. As political tensions drove England and the colonies farther and farther apart, ecclesiastical tensions fanned the flames. English bishops were merely another instance of English power—except that by 1770 colonists spoke not of power but of tyranny. That tyranny, civil and ecclesiastic, was a single tyranny to be resisted in a single drive for independence, civil and ecclesiastic. The attempt to bring Anglican bishops to America, wrote one Presbyterian layman in 1768, was of one piece with the attempt, by way of the Stamp Act, to tax America. Both must be resisted by "every man who sets a proper value either on his liberty, property, or conscience."

Outside Virginia, feelings against Anglican demands and the often assumed Anglican loyalty to England ran even higher. In 1776 a Church of England missionary in Pennsylvania declared,

> I have been obliged to shut my Churches to avoid the fury of the populace who would not suffer the Liturgy to be used unless the Collects and Prayers for the King & Royal Family were omitted. . . . Indeed, every clergyman of the Church of England who dared to act upon proper principles was marked out for infamy and insult. . . . Some of them have been dragged from their horses, assaulted with stones & dirt, ducked in water; obliged to flee for their lives, driven from their habitations & families, laid under arrests & imprisoned!

Happily, passions in Virginia did not run so high, mainly because the laity in the Anglican churches were generally favorable to the American cause and resistant to the idea of a bishop in their midst. Moreover, the parishes were governed by leading laymen who sat on the vestries. In the absence of a bishop, they exercised more authority over community morality and behavior than did the resident clergy. Most of these vestrymen had no desire to share this authority or see it diminished by the sudden arrival of a bishop. Moreover, as Anglican layman Richard Bland indicated in 1771, any hope of religious

Members of Virginia's Anglican churches, such as Bruton Parish in Williamsburg, generally opposed efforts to establish bishoprics in America.

harmony in Virginia would be permanently shattered if England should send over one or more bishops. And let me tell you, Bland added, that "a religious dispute is the most fierce and destructive of all others to the peace and happiness of government."

For a decade or two before the American Revolution, the Anglican church in Virginia had the opportunity to participate in the Great Awakening, to join with the dissenters in promoting an evangelical religion of broad appeal to all levels and races and conditions of society. Instead, the Church of England chose to hold itself aloof from these newer religious movements (Devereux Jarratt being the exception) and to seek a tighter relationship with ecclesiastical and political authorities in England. It was a fateful decision. When the Revolution did erupt, Anglicanism suffered while the dissenting groups prospered. What had started as a dispute over bishops ended as a dispute over patriotism and loyalty.

An American Episcopal Church

In 1785 Virginia's English church formally reorganized as the Protestant Episcopal Church in the United States of America. Its prayer book was revised to eliminate those prayers for English royalty that American patriots in Pennsylvania and elsewhere had found so offensive. Now Episcopalians could elect their own bishops as purely spiritual officers without political authority and without the involvement of England. Calling upon its friends and members not "to abandon it in the hour of difficulty," the Episcopal church took steps to recover from "the more than eight years our church hath languished under neglect." The newly elected bishop of this church in Virginia saw around him nothing but ruin and despair. Enemies threatened from the outside, while indifference threatened from within. Where to begin in the process of rebuilding, both buildings and hearts? It was imperative, he declared, to improve church attendance, to increase voluntary contributions, and to rescue houses of worship from disrepair and collapse. "I know that inattention to religion produces indifference," the bishop stated, "and that indifference terminates in irreligion, in profaneness, and impiety."

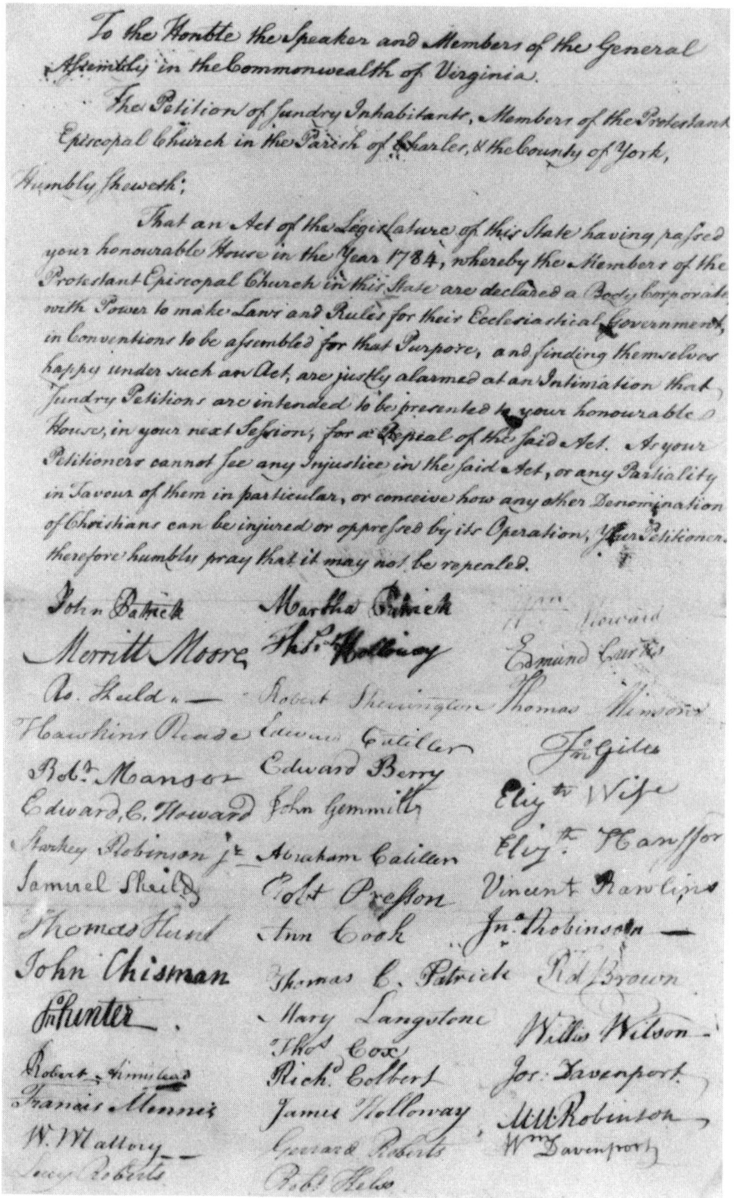

To the Honble the Speaker and Members of the General Assembly in the Commonwealth of Virginia.

The Petition of sundry Inhabitants, Members of the Protestant Episcopal Church in the Parish of Charles, & the County of York,

Humbly sheweth;

That an Act of the Legislature of this State having passed your honourable House in the Year 1784, whereby the Members of the Protestant Episcopal Church in this State are declared a Body corporate with Power to make Laws and Rules for their Ecclesiastical Government, in Conventions to be assembled for that Purpose, and finding themselves happy under such an Act, are justly alarmed at an Intimation that sundry Petitions are intended to be presented to your honourable House, in your next Session, for a Repeal of the said Act. As your Petitioners cannot see any Injustice in the said Act, or any Partiality in Favour of them in particular, or conceive how any other Denomination of Christians can be injured or oppressed by its Operation, Your Petitioners therefore humbly pray that it may not be repealed.

John Patrick
Martha Patrick
Merritt Moore
Thos. Holloway
Edmund Curtis
Ro. Sheild
Robert Sherrington
Thomas Wilson
Hawkins Reade
Edward Cabiller
Jno. Giles
Robt. Manson
Edward Berry
Eliz. Wise
Edward C. Howard
John Gemmill
Eliz. Hansford
Starkey Robinson jr.
Abraham Cabiller
Vincent Rawlins
Samuel Sheild
Robt. Presson
Jno. Robinson
Thomas Hunt
Ann Cook
Robt. Brown
John Chisman
Thomas C. Patrick
Jno. Hunter
Mary Langstone
Willis Wilson
Thos. Cox
Jos. Davenport
Robert Hamilton
Richd. Colbert
Francis Mennis
James Holloway
W. W. Robinson
W. Mallory
Gerard Roberts
Wm. Davenport
Lucy Roberts
Robt. Hobs

In December 1786, members of the Protestant Episcopal Church in Charles Parish of York County petitioned the Virginia Assembly not to repeal the act establishing the denomination. *Courtesy, Virginia State Library and Archives.*

The years of difficulty were not over, however, as legal disputes and unrelenting attacks kept the now-Americanized church on the defensive. Enemies continued to view with suspicion or hostility every move made by a once-powerful denomination suddenly shorn of all its official power.

Post-Revolutionary Opposition to Establishment

Since, as has been noted above, an established church was thoroughly mixed with politics, society, and culture, it was difficult to disestablish Anglicanism all at once. Laws had to be changed, customs had to be challenged, judicial opinions had to be rendered, and the voices of all the people had to be heard. Toleration had been achieved by 1776; religious freedom had not. The latter would not be achieved until every lingering hint of favoritism toward one particular church was removed and every civil liability respecting all other churches obliterated. With the Revolution won by 1783, Virginia's Presbyterians made clear the very next year just what that victory meant in their eyes—namely, "An entire and everlasting freedom from every species of ecclesiastical domination, and private judgment, and an equal share of the protection and favor of government to all denominations of Christians." Later that same year, 1784, the Baptists used equally strong language as they called upon Virginia's legislators to do away with "all distinctions in your laws" to the end that "no order or denomination of Christians in this Commonwealth have any Separate Privileges allowed them, more than their Brethren of other Religious Societies . . . lest they Tyrannize over them."

Baptist clergy especially objected to laws still in effect that made it illegal for them to perform marriages outside their own counties, "even among Members of their own Societies and Congregations." Since the Episcopal vestry still used tax money for local charity and welfare, but only Episcopalians could sit on the vestry, this too seemed rankest discrimination against all non-Episcopalians. In this fashion, the Baptists pointed out, "the property of Dissenters is taken from them by those who are not their Representatives." A long war had been fought over the principle of no taxation without representation; it seemed a good principle to apply to religion as well. Methodists, busy transforming themselves into a separate denomination in 1784, nonetheless took time to make common cause with the Presbyterians and the Baptists. Not only were they not represented, the Methodists noted, but they along with many others were treated still as though they were "illiterate Zealots."

In addition to these dissenting Christians, a small but powerful group of political leaders influenced by the eighteenth-century Enlightenment, also called the Age of Reason, spoke out against the established church and its privileged position. While these men were few, they weighed heavily in the fortunes of both the state and the nation, as the names of Thomas Jefferson and James Madison immediately suggest. These Virginia statesmen also believed in and argued for full religious freedom, though they stood on different theological grounds from the Baptists, Methodists, and Presbyterians. Jefferson and Madison believed that when the power of the church was joined with the power of the state, the resulting combination worked to the detriment of both state and church and also to the injury of the people at large. Besides, as Jefferson observed in his *Notes on Virginia,* no genuine church had to be propped up by military or civil power: "It is error alone which needs the support of government. Truth can stand by itself."

Thomas Jefferson.

Jefferson, Madison, and others of like mind, sometimes called deists, were not hostile to religion, but they were hostile to politically powerful, politically ambitious religion. Deists were not hostile to theology, but they were hostile to any theology derived from biblical revelation rather than from nature and reason. For the deists, an established church was by its very nature a roadblock to the progress of civilization and an invitation to superstition and intellectual surrender. Anglicanism as supported in Virginia and several other colonies, Congregationalism as supported in New England—these churches were the special objects of deist condemnation. Official religions such as these—backed by whips, jails, and fines—provoked Jefferson later to write that he had "sworn upon the altar of God, eternal hostility against every form of tyranny over the mind of man." Together, Jefferson and Madison would labor to purge Virginia of such tyranny.

The Anglican Counterattack

The Anglican fortress did not fall quickly or easily. Powerful civil and religious leaders still favored the traditional link between the church and the state. All Western nations, these proponents argued, had found it wisest and safest to join these two powerful institutions. Ever since the fourth century, when Constantine made Christianity the official religion of the Roman Empire, all rulers had believed religious establishment to be essential to the health of society, the stability of the state, the orthodoxy of the clergy, and the prosperity of the church. Such, at least, was the argument of Virginia's Anglican clergy before the Revolution, during the war, and immediately after. One Anglican minister, traveling into the western regions of the South in 1766, reported that society and religion there were in total disarray. The Church of England had less effective control in the Piedmont and backcountry than in the Tidewater; as a result, this Anglican declared, what goes on in the frontier "tabernacles" hardly deserved to be called religion. It was, rather, "the Scandal of Religion and Insult of Common Sense." To this minister, the backcountry was proof enough that Anglicanism must be supported and advanced by the state; otherwise, Christianity would be "scandalized and brought into Contempt," devotion would be ridiculed, and religion itself would ultimately collapse. Church and state, therefore, should continue to work hand in hand—despite revolution, despite dissent, despite such "modern" thinkers as Jefferson and Madison.

In the early 1780s, many prominent Virginia families, especially in the eastern regions, argued that a political revolution did not demand an ecclesiastical one as well. Since 1619 Virginia had enjoyed the blessings of an established church, they pointed out. Why should that long and honored tradition be suddenly and rudely abandoned? Leaders such as Edmund Pendleton and Robert Carter Nicholas argued that a continuing connection between church and state was not only good for Virginia ("conducive to peace and happiness"), but also constituted simple justice for those clergy who had made lifetime commitments to the Church of England. Agreements made in good faith before the Revolution should be honored even after that Revolution. While these arguments had some appeal throughout the state, dissenters and deists were by 1784 too strong to allow a single denomination, no matter how long its history or how powerful its precedent, to enjoy special privileges or protections above all others.

When it became obvious that the Church of England could not continue in its unique status, the pro-establishment forces fell back to a second line of defense. They argued that Chris-

Patrick Henry.

tianity itself should become the state's official religion, rather than any single denomination. Patrick Henry, the powerful patriotic orator, took the lead in proposing that "the Christian religion shall in all times coming be deemed and held to be the established Religion of this Commonwealth; and all Denominations of Christians demeaning themselves peaceably and faithfully shall enjoy equal privileges." Under this proposal, all persons who had been taxed for the support of the Anglican church would now be taxed for the support of the State's official version of Christianity. A "general assessment" would thus be levied on all taxpayers, church members or no. Henry, son of an Anglican father and a Presbyterian mother (he had often heard Samuel Davies preach), believed that many of the dissenters could be persuaded to support this broad proposal. For now they, too, and not Anglicanism alone, could benefit from state assistance and protection.

General Assessment and Madison's "Memorial"

Among most dissenters, however, Henry's "general assessment bill" (as it came to be called) found little favor. Baptists continued to resist all governmental meddling in religion, whether it be on their own behalf or on the behalf of others. In 1784 they expressed to the Virginia legislature their fervent wish "that every grievous yoke be broken . . . and that in every Act, the bright beams of equal Liberty and Impartial Justice may shine." In that same year, Virginia's Presbyterians, to Henry's keen disappointment, declared that his proposed establishment of the Christian religion was unwise, unnecessary, and "a direct violation of the [Virginia] Declaration of Rights." The legislature, they continued, must recognize its own limits and refrain from asserting a "Supremacy in Spirituals." Patrick Henry, joined by such influential figures as Richard Henry Lee and John Marshall, pressed on in his campaign to establish Christianity. But the opposition continued to grow, much of it ably directed by James Madison.

A member of the Virginia legislature with Henry, Madison labored and lobbied hard against the very notion of a "general assessment." But to defeat a bill that had so much argument from history and tradition behind it required more than skillful political maneuver. All the force of logic and persuasive argument was also required. This Madison provided most elo-

Richard Henry Lee. Courtesy, The City Archives of Philadelphia.

quently in 1785 in a now famous document entitled "Memorial and Remonstrance." The "memorial" was a petition to the legislature, while the "remonstrance" was a protest against the bill proposed by Patrick Henry.

In this carefully written statement, Madison argued that religion could never properly be a matter of law, something to be enforced by the police or the courts or the prisons. On the contrary, Madison asserted, religion "can be directed only be reason and conviction." This being the case, neither governors nor legislators had the right or authority—much less the wisdom—to "judge of Religious Truth." If today we agree that the state can legitimately establish Christianity, Madison reasoned, then tomorrow we can with equal lawfulness establish "any particular sect of Christians, in exclusion of all other Sects." This, as Madison's readers could easily see, would return Virginia to the control of a single, official church. Beyond all this, Madison revealed his own passionate conviction that the alliance between church and state had, throughout history, proved to be a disaster for both. During almost fifteen hundred years of such close alliance, "What have been its fruits?" Madison asked. His reply: "More or less in all places, pride and indolence in the Clegy, ignorance and servility in the laity; in both, superstition, bigotry, and persecution." We shall be true to the principles of "the late Revolution," Madison concluded, not by constricting the bands of freedom, but by widening them. We must preserve Virginia and indeed the whole nation as "an Asylum to the persecuted," leaving all laws about religion to the only truly qualified authority in this area, "the Supreme Lawgiver of the Universe."

Thomas Jefferson's Bill

Under the force of such argument, the Virginia legislators turned away from further consideration of how religion should be favored to reflect on how it might be made more free. At last they were ready to vote on Jefferson's long-delayed "Bill for Establishing Religious Freedom." Though Jefferson had written the bill in 1777, the legislature had failed to give it a favorable hearing at any time during the Revolution. Now, three years after the war had ended, the time had come to complete the political revolution with an ecclesiastical one.

Though Jefferson was the new nation's minister to France in 1786, Madison was again ready to lead the battle on the floor of the Virginia legislature. The bill was debated, amended, discussed some more, and ultimately passed early that year. A landmark in the history of religious freedom (as a monument erected in Fredericksburg appropriately recognizes), the bill affirmed,

> [N]o man shall be compelled to frequent or support any religious worship, place or ministry whatsoever, nor shall be enforced, restrained, molested, or burthened in his body or goods, nor shall otherwise suffer, on account of his religious opinions or belief, but that all men shall be free to profess, and by argument to maintain, their opinions in matters of religion, and the same shall in no wise diminish, enlarge, or affect their civil capacities.

Inscription on Thomas Jefferson's tombstone. *Courtesy, Monticello/Thomas Jefferson Memorial Foundation, Inc.*

The pivotal and populous state of Virginia, having supported the oldest church establishment in America, now took the boldest step away from all establishment toward a full and unrestricted freedom in religion. Jefferson, too, saw this bill as a landmark. He asked that only two of his writings be noted on his tombstone: the Declaration of Independence, adopted by his nation in 1776, and the Statute for Establishing Religious Freedom, adopted by his state a decade later.

Virginia and the Constitution

While legislators in Richmond were giving their final approval to Jefferson's bill in 1786, delegates from New Hampshire to Georgia were being selected to attend an important convention to gather in Philadelphia in May 1787. That convention, called to amend or revise the Articles of Confederation, ended by writing an entirely new instrument of government, which we now know as the Constitution of the United States. When the delegates came to the subject of religion, they had the principles laid down by Jefferson and Madison very much on their minds. As a result, the Constitution itself said little about religion; it was simply not the business of government to involve itself with religion. Consequently, the Constitution declared nothing about establishing one denomination or all denominations, nothing about a national creed, a national clergy, a national church. In Virginia the task had been to do away with an established church long in place; in Philadelphia the task was to prevent any establishment from coming into being. At the end of that long, hot Philadelphia summer, the framers of the Constitution therefore contented themselves with a single phrase relevant to religion: "no religious Test shall ever be required as a Qualification to any Office or public Trust under the United States" (Article VI). In other words, religion could never be used either as a qualification or a disqualification for any elective or appointive office within the federal government.

Some Americans doubted that such a brief statement was sufficient to protect the religious freedom of all citizens, whether officeholders or not. Religious liberty was so dear and its violation so terrible that stronger and clearer language might well be needed. Here again the leadership of Virginia was critical. Madison, often called the "father of the Constitution," was active at every stage of drafting the document and encouraging its ratification by the people in all thirteen states. He was naturally concerned also to know what his good friend Thomas Jefferson thought about it in faraway Paris. As soon as the work in Philadelphia was finished, Madison sent a copy of the Constitution to Jefferson.

Thomas Jefferson on the whole approved of what Madison and the other delegates had done, but he thought the stand taken on behalf of fundamental liberties was not strong enough. "I will now add what I do not like," Jefferson wrote to Madison in December of 1787. "First, the omission of a bill of rights providing clearly . . . for freedom of religion, freedom of the press, protection against standing armies," and several other basic rights. Jefferson was convinced that such liberties could not be left to chance and interpretation, or to changing administrations and changing times. Thus Jefferson along with many others urged that the Constitution, if ratified, be immediately amended with a Bill of Rights. Once again, Madison agreed to lead this vital endeavor, no longer as a member of Virginia's Assembly but as a newly elected representative to the first Congress under the Constitution. On September 25, 1789, the United States Congress set forth the first ten amendments for approval; by the end of 1791, they had become part of the Constitution.

On the list of rights Jefferson sent to Madison, religious freedom emerged as his first concern. And when Congress passed its Bill of Rights, religion once more preceded all other guarantees. The first part of the First Amendment reads, "Congress shall make no law respecting an establishment of religion, or prohibiting the free exercise thereof." It was a double protection: first, Congress shall do nothing to favor, support, or promote religion; second, Congress shall do nothing to interfere with or control or suppress religion. Neither hinder nor help—the government must simply leave religion alone. Jefferson had so argued in 1777; the Virginia legislature had so voted in 1786; now, in 1791, it had become the policy of all the nation on behalf of all the people. The familiar phrase, "wall of separa-

James Madison.

tion between church and state," is not in the Constitution, but it is Jeffersonian. Using that expression in a letter written while he was President, Jefferson revealed his own hope that the First Amendment would be interpreted with great strictness and meticulous care. Long after he left the Presidency, Jefferson continued to warn against what he called "this loathsome combination of church and state."

Evangelical Religion after the Revolution

Those forces most interested in promoting religious freedom were best able to take advantage of it. In Virginia after 1786, those who had previously been known as dissenters—Presbyterians, Methodists, Baptists—no longer faced legal barriers to the growth and expansion of their own churches. Just as surely as the nation of England had lost the Revolution, so the Church of England had lost its legal struggle in Virginia to maintain its privileges and protection. It needed time to reorganize, rethink, and regroup. The evangelical forces, on the other hand, seized the moment to make the decades of the 1780s and 1790s a time of great expansion, so much so that by 1800 these three groups dominated the state. And as in the Great Awakening of decades before, these churches emphasized a gospel of salvation, a personal commitment to a new fellowship, and a conscious striving for high standards in morality and purity in doctrine.

This striking increase in evangelical religion is emphatically not to be understood in terms of white males alone. Southern women in this period became increasingly prominent not merely as church members but as leaders in much of church life. If men clearly dominated in the political and commercial realms, women—often considered both more pious and more moral than most men—assumed an ever-increasing role in religion. In Virginia as well as elsewhere in the South, women took seriously their obligation to instill in their children a loyalty to the doctrinal and ethical teachings of their churches. The dispensing of charity, formerly the province of Anglican vestries, now often fell under the direction and watchful eyes of the church women. Women were also responsible for the maintenance of church buildings and for the welfare of the clergy, duties that had once been government projects. Except among the Quakers, women did not generally become clergy nor regularly speak in public assemblies; nonetheless, within the churches themselves, their authority and impact steadily increased.

Even more dramatic was the spread of evangelical religion among Virginia's black men and women who, in 1800, constituted about 40 percent of the state's total population of eight hundred thousand. Blacks turned in largest numbers toward the Baptists, but in significant force they also became Methodists and Presbyterians. Some black men and women joined predominantly white churches, but more often African-Americans formed their own fellowships. As early as 1758 African-Americans established their own church in Mecklenburg; other churches soon followed in Williamsburg, Richmond, and Petersburg. On some occasions a black preacher led a congregation that was racially integrated. In Portsmouth, Virginia, for example, when the white minister resigned in 1792, the congregation of whites and blacks chose a talented black preacher, Josiah (or Jacob) Bishop, as its new pastor. So effective did Bishop prove to be that the congregation managed to purchase his freedom and that of his entire family.

An interpreter portrays an African-American preacher at Colonial Williamsburg.

Among Baptists, black or white, the chief qualification for the ministry was a demonstrated "gift" of preaching or exhorting in such a way as to win approval and draw a following. Such a gift, assumed to be God-given, was, therefore, more than merely human talent; it was a divine sanction or call. When a slave named Simon manifested such a call, the Roanoke Baptist Association purchased his freedom in 1792 so that he might have full liberty to exercise that gift. In Gloucester County, Nottoway County, and elsewhere, early records testify to the active ministry of black Baptists. In at least two instances, at Petersburg and Williamsburg, black Baptists organized congregations before white Baptists did. And in the large First Baptist Church in Richmond, the integrated congregation had a choice among as many as five black preachers.

The recently organized Methodist denomination also encouraged preaching by blacks. Indeed, one free Negro, Henry Evans, carried the Methodist message into portions of North Carolina even before any white Methodists had arrived. Presbyterians in 1801 appointed a free black, John Chavis, to serve specifically as a missionary in Virginia and North Carolina to "people of his own color." It often happened, however, that blacks preaching to blacks attracted large numbers of whites as well, so that evangelical religion seemed for a time to ignore many racial boundaries. Unhappily, that time did not last.

By the 1830s the forces of abolition on the one hand and the defenders of slavery on the other raised emotions to such a height that easy association between the races became more the exception than the rule. Laws were passed that forbade blacks preaching or gathering in large crowds. Black churches were frequently closed down for fear of slave rebellions. In 1831 black exhorter Nat Turner from Southampton, Virginia, led the bloodiest slave revolt of all. Claiming to have been called to such action by God, Turner aroused great fear among slave owners throughout the South. Black religion had been seen by many whites as a means for keeping slaves submissive and obedient, but Turner's example now revealed that the sword of the spirit had a sharper edge.

Religion among African-Americans was indeed double-edged, as Willie Lee Rose has noted: "It brought forth both Nat Turners and Uncle Toms [but] in either case it caused slaves to *think.*" It also enabled blacks, as it had whites, to create new and intimate churches wherein all were "brothers" and "sisters," where none was under arbitrary human authority, but under the authority only of the Bible and God. With a common vocabulary, a common understanding of the way in which God worked in the affairs of men and women, a common expectation regarding a "promised land" for which all earnest Christians were bound—with this fresh world view whites and blacks, females and males, slaves and free people fundamentally transformed the nature of Virginia society from that which had prevailed throughout most of the seventeenth and eighteenth centuries. In one unbending and tragic respect, however, Virginia society in the early 1800s remained inflexible.

Religion and the Institution of Slavery

Despite the strong criticism that evangelical religion leveled against slavery, the institution would not yield. Indeed, its defense became stronger and more strident. As previously noted, John Leland in 1790 spoke of slavery as being "pregnant with enormous evils." Six years before that, the Methodists in Frederick County declared that personal liberty was the birthright of every rational creature without exception; this being so, the Methodists petitioned the Virginia legislature "to pursue the most Prudential, but effectual Method" for getting rid of slavery. (See Appendix B.) The Quakers in Virginia, as elsewhere, maintained the most consistent pressure against allowing slavery to continue in time or expand in territory. In 1782 Virginia Quakers succeeded in passing a law that permitted individual slave owners to free their slaves, but in 1806 new restrictions on manumission effectively closed this avenue to freedom.

By the 1830s evangelical religion in America no longer spoke with one voice on this issue. It ceased, therefore, to be an effective counterweight to the ever-increasing economic and political pressures to maintain the South's "peculiar institution" undiminished in any way. Methodists in the South denounced abolitionism as a "false philosophy" that set aside the Scriptures, while their co-religionists in the North described slavery as a "flagrant violation of the law of God." It was not possible to maintain such sharply contrasting views indefinitely in a single denomination. In 1844, therefore, Methodists split apart with the Methodist Episcopal Church, South, going its separate way

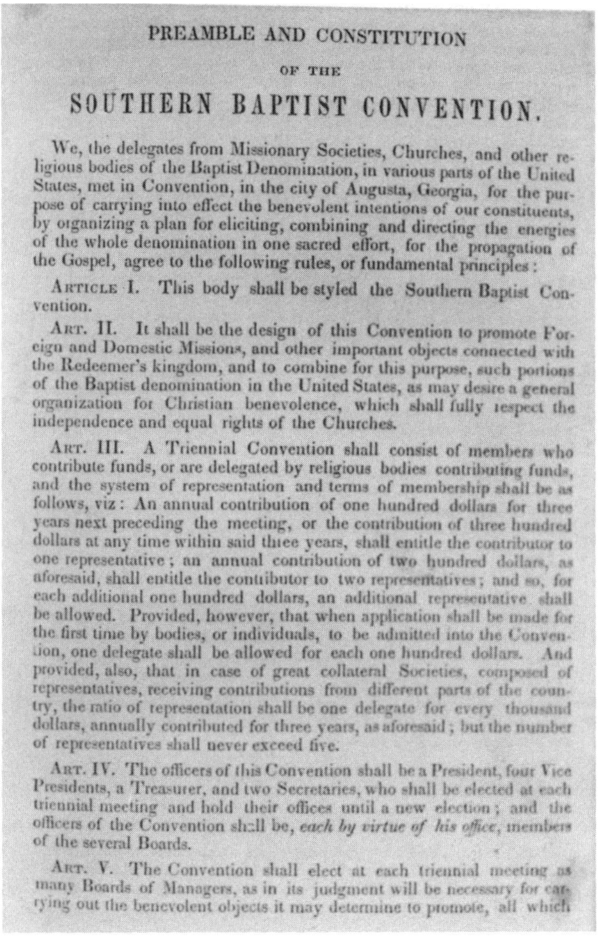
PREAMBLE AND CONSTITUTION

OF THE

SOUTHERN BAPTIST CONVENTION.

We, the delegates from Missionary Societies, Churches, and other religious bodies of the Baptist Denomination, in various parts of the United States, met in Convention, in the city of Augusta, Georgia, for the purpose of carrying into effect the benevolent intentions of our constituents, by organizing a plan for eliciting, combining and directing the energies of the whole denomination in one sacred effort, for the propagation of the Gospel, agree to the following rules, or fundamental principles:

ARTICLE I. This body shall be styled the Southern Baptist Convention.

ART. II. It shall be the design of this Convention to promote Foreign and Domestic Missions, and other important objects connected with the Redeemer's kingdom, and to combine for this purpose, such portions of the Baptist denomination in the United States, as may desire a general organization for Christian benevolence, which shall fully respect the independence and equal rights of the Churches.

ART. III. A Triennial Convention shall consist of members who contribute funds, or are delegated by religious bodies contributing funds, and the system of representation and terms of membership shall be as follows, viz: An annual contribution of one hundred dollars for three years next preceding the meeting, or the contribution of three hundred dollars at any time within said three years, shall entitle the contributor to one representative; an annual contribution of two hundred dollars, as aforesaid, shall entitle the contributor to two representatives; and so, for each additional one hundred dollars, an additional representative shall be allowed. Provided, however, that when application shall be made for the first time by bodies, or individuals, to be admitted into the Convention, one delegate shall be allowed for each one hundred dollars. And provided, also, that in case of great collateral Societies, composed of representatives, receiving contributions from different parts of the country, the ratio of representation shall be one delegate for every thousand dollars, annually contributed for three years, as aforesaid; but the number of representatives shall never exceed five.

ART. IV. The officers of this Convention shall be a President, four Vice Presidents, a Treasurer, and two Secretaries, who shall be elected at each triennial meeting and hold their offices until a new election; and the officers of the Convention shall be, *each by virtue of his office*, members of the several Boards.

ART. V. The Convention shall elect at each triennial meeting as many Boards of Managers, as in its judgment will be necessary for carrying out the benevolent objects it may determine to promote, all which

Constitution of the Southern Baptist Convention, May 8, 1845.
Courtesy, Virginia Baptist Historical Society.

from the parent body in the North. Baptists likewise found themselves bitterly divided, with those in the South arguing that "the right of holding slaves is clearly established in the Holy Scriptures, both by precept and example." Elsewhere, Baptists spoke of slavery, even in its best state, as "a violation of man's nature and the Christian law of love." That denomination too, one year after the Methodists, separated into southern and northern branches. The Southern Baptist Convention no longer affiliated itself with national boards and societies that once had served all Baptists. Just before the Civil War, Presbyterians also divided, north and south, as slavery became the issue that above all others split not only churches but the nation itself.

In Virginia these divisions meant that no powerful organization stood in unified opposition to slavery, just as no powerful voice such as Jefferson's or Madison's was raised in forthright condemnation of the institution. Around 1800, it might have been possible to eliminate slavery in Virginia through appeals to reason and justice and mercy. By 1850, emancipation could no longer be discussed in calm and rational tones. Sides had been chosen, positions had hardened, and religion had been relegated to the sidelines, where it proved powerless to prevent the approaching battle.

Robert Carter III and a New Religion

At the end of the eighteenth century, Robert Carter III, wealthy plantation owner and slaveholder, set his own slaves free. He did so not in the name of evangelical religion but under the inspiration of a novel religious body recently arrived in America. As a young man, Carter (grandson of the better known Robert "King" Carter) grew up in the fold of the Anglican church with which all of his family had been affiliated. After graduating from the College of William and Mary, young Carter journeyed to London to further his cultural development. Returning to Virginia in 1751, he took his expected place in the colonial power structure as the head of his large plantation at Nomini Hall. At this point, one might logically have assumed that Robert Carter III would join those most determined to maintain the position of the Church of England in Revolutionary Virginia. But in 1777 Carter had a deep personal religious experience during which he felt suddenly relieved of the burdens of sin and guilt, lifted up by virtue of God's performing "a mighty work of my soul." A year later, in a period of intense religious activity, Carter participated in many prayer meetings and evangelistic services. Then on September 6, 1778, he made a public confession of his newfound Christian faith, was baptized by immersion, and joined the Baptist church in his home county of Westmoreland.

This surprising step for an Anglican gentleman was not the end of Carter's spiritual journey. He continued to search for satisfying answers to the ever-larger cosmic questions that he asked. He wished to know more of the universe and of his precise place in it. Eleven years after becoming a Baptist, Carter left that fellowship to identify with the Church of the New

Robert Carter III of Nomini Hall. *Courtesy, Virginia Historical Society.*

Jerusalem. Also called Swedenborgianism (after its European founder, Emanuel Swedenborg, 1688–1772), this new religion spoke of healing, compassion, reconciliation, innocence, charity, and a love between man and woman that continued even after death. Just as Carter had earlier endeavored to be a conciliator in the political realm, so he now assumed a leading role in a church that, he believed, could bring peace to strife-torn Virginia, peace among all churches as well as between the races. Beginning the gradual manumission of his five hundred slaves in 1791, Carter also sought peace within his own anxious and restless soul. When he died in 1804, his private pilgrimage over, his religious quest had stimulated no mass movement among his fellow Virginians. Robert Carter of Nomini Hall personified only an intimate and earnest search for genuine spiritual understanding and rest within.

Thomas Jefferson and Rational Religion

When it came to religion, Thomas Jefferson chose to listen much more to reason than to revelation or dogma or powerful church leaders. Though he remained within the Anglican church all his life, Jefferson rejected both the doctrine and the authority of the Church of England. He did not reject Christianity, but he believed that this religion had been distorted during the centuries since Jesus. The moral system of Jesus, Jefferson declared in 1803, "was the most benevolent and sublime probably that has been ever taught." The problem, he felt, was that this moral teaching had been so encumbered and garbled by churches and priests that no one knew what Jesus had really said. Jefferson, determined to correct that situation, spent many hours with his New Testaments in Greek, French, Latin, and English so that he could present "The Life and Morals of Jesus" in uncorrupted form. "The sum of all religion," Jefferson wrote in 1816, was expressed by its best preacher: "Fear God and love thy neighbor."

Like his fellow deists, Jefferson believed that God spoke to His creatures not in Hebrew or Greek but in the language of nature. We know who or what God is, the deists argued, by observing closely the world that He made. Reason, not revelation, was for all deists the only possible path to truth. And the truly religious life had far more to do with morality and virtue than with theology and dogma. Jefferson declared that if he were to found a new sect, his fundamental principle "would be the reverse of Calvin's, that we are saved by our good works which are within our power, and not by our faith which is not within our power." So confident was Jefferson in the power of reason and of rational religion that he predicted that all Americans, within a generation or two, would turn to Unitarianism.

Though at one point Jefferson observed that he was "of a sect by myself, as far as I know," at other times he was will-

Works such as Joseph Priestley's History of the Corruptions of Christianity *influenced Jefferson's views on religion.* *Courtesy, Library of Congress.*

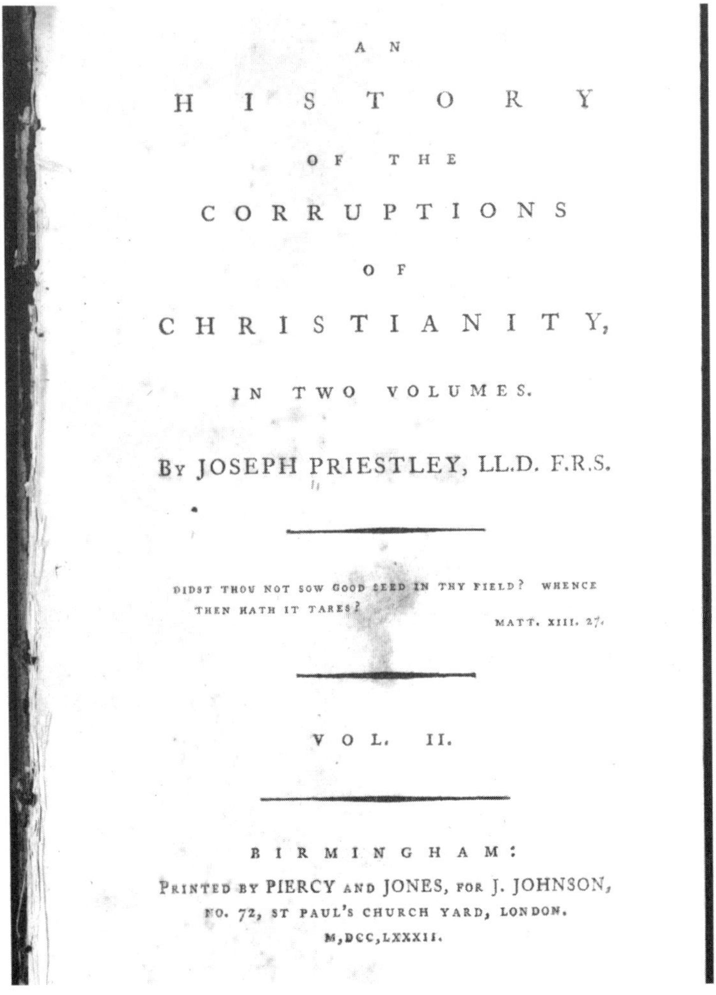
AN

HISTORY

OF THE

CORRUPTIONS

OF

CHRISTIANITY,

IN TWO VOLUMES.

BY JOSEPH PRIESTLEY, LL.D. F.R.S.

DIDST THOU NOT SOW GOOD SEED IN THY FIELD? WHENCE THEN HATH IT TARES?

MATT. XIII. 27.

VOL. II.

BIRMINGHAM:

PRINTED BY PIERCY AND JONES, FOR J. JOHNSON, NO. 72, ST PAUL'S CHURCH YARD, LONDON.

M,DCC,LXXXII.

ing to call himself a Christian, "that is to say, a disciple of the doctrines of Jesus, very different from the Platonists." Christian theology in the third and fourth centuries, Jefferson believed, had taken on too much Greek philosophy, thereby exchanging simplicity for mystery. Jesus, in Jefferson's view, was not divine, nor did he ever claim divinity for himself. The idea of Jesus as the Son of God was, for Jefferson, another of those Platonic mysteries that orthodox Christianity had promoted for centuries. He called the doctrine of the Trinity "mere Abacadabra." The religion of Jesus himself, Jefferson noted in 1820, "is founded on the unity of God." Jefferson's hostility to institutional religion, as opposed to rational religion, led him to the great achievement of his final years—the founding of an educational institution free of all sectarian control.

Virginia's Modern University

When Jefferson was governor of Virginia (1779–1781), he began laying plans for a university that would differ markedly from all those then in existence in America. It would be several decades, however, before those plans bore visible fruit. The great problem with higher education in America, Jefferson believed, was that it was largely under the control of sectarian religion. Harvard, Yale, and Dartmouth were dominated by the Congregationalists; Princeton by the Presbyterians; Columbia as well as William and Mary by the Anglicans; and Brown by the Baptists. At the beginning of the nineteenth century, no state had more than one university, and Virginia of course already had its institution of higher learning—the College of William and Mary, founded in 1693 as the second oldest college in the country. Why would Jefferson propose that Virginia have an additional university?

The answer lay in the strong Anglican flavor that continued to permeate William and Mary, his own alma mater. The college was founded to train Anglican ministers; the faculty consisted largely of Anglican ministers; the students and faculty alike had to pledge their loyalty to Anglicanism and its creed. As the college statutes of 1728 had declared: "The Founders of this College proposed to themselves . . . that the Churches of America, especially Virginia, should be supplied with good

Ministers after the Doctrine and Government of the Church of England; and that the College should be a constant Seminary for this Purpose." The Revolution produced no clean break between the college and the church, and therefore Jefferson was unwilling to make this Anglican school the major state university of Virginia. When he retired from the Presidency of the United States in 1809, he gave major attention to creating a new and truly *public* university. William and Mary, he wrote to a friend, "must descend into the secondary rank of academies of preparation for the University."

Population was increasing in the western part of Virginia, as indicated by the relocation of the state's capital from Williamsburg to Richmond in 1780. Jefferson decided that his university should also be in the western part of the state, away from the Anglican-dominated Tidewater. Where better, then, than near his own home, Monticello, where he could directly supervise every aspect of its creation? He chose a site in Charlottesville, laid out the grounds, raised the funds, purchased books for the library, designed the curriculum, and selected the faculty.

The University of Virginia was to have professorships in languages and law, natural and moral philosophy, history, mathematics, and medicine—but no professor of divinity. Jefferson explained, "In conformity with the principles of our constitution, which places all sects of religion on an equal footing, with the jealousies of the different sects in guarding that equality from encroachment & surprise, and with the sentiments of the legislature in favor of freedom of religion on former occasions, we have proposed no professor of Divinity." For the sake of religious freedom, his university would be free of religion. Also, for the sake of an education that would be "broad & liberal & modern," Jefferson would keep the clergy far away; he believed them to be the enemies of serious education, interested more in casting "spells on the human mind" than in promoting its improvement.

In 1825, the university in Charlottesville opened its doors to sixty-eight students. Jefferson, one year before his death, had the great pleasure of presiding as rector over those opening ceremonies. And on his tombstone, he wished to be remembered for one more deed beyond composing the Declaration of Independence and the Statute for Establishing Religion Freedom—namely, the founding of the University of Virginia.

The Rotunda at the University of Virginia. © *University of Virginia.*

Summary

By the time of Jefferson's death in 1826, religion and society and politics in Virginia would hardly have been recognizable to one who had lived in the royal colony a mere hundred years before. In the first quarter of the eighteenth century, the Church of England and England's will prevailed over all those lands bordering the Chesapeake as well as along those great rivers so important to Virginia's early development, the Potomac, Rappahannock, York, and James. Dissent was but a small cloud on the horizon, revivalism a phenomenon unknown, revolution against the mother country an unthinkable prospect, and freedom of religion the vision of only a few fanatics farther north.

In less than a century, Virginia's world had been turned upside-down. Religious variety took the place of religious conformity, as German congregations, Quaker meetings, and evangelical churches spread from the western mountains to the Atlantic Ocean and back again. Revivalism thrust religion out of the sacred sanctuaries into the open fields and market places; it also opened the ranks of the ministry to the masses, black and white, learned and simple. Revolution challenged the authority of bishops, lords, and kings, that challenge finding its convincing success at Yorktown in 1781. One decade later, the new nation had its Constitution and Bill of Rights, ensuring that the challenge to tyranny would endure and that long and bloody persecutions for religious belief would end. When in 1825 Virginia opened its free and liberal university, the first permanent English colony had been transformed into a modern American state.

Appendix A

George Whitefield in Virginia, 1739

Friday, Dec. 14. Left Colonel Whiting's about seven in the morning, and passed through Gloucester Town, a very small place. Crossed a ferry a mile wide. Dined at York and reached Williamsburgh, the metropolis of Virginia, by the evening. The gentleman before mentioned kindly accompanied us; with him I discoursed much on the things pertaining to the Kingdom of God. He seemed to be one to whom God had given a hearing ear and an obedient heart. I have not met with a temper more resembling that of Nathaniel for a great while. Oh that the Lord would make him an Israelite indeed! [See John 1:45–51]

Saturday, Dec. 15. Waited on and afterwards (at his invitation) dined with the Governor, who received me most courteously. Paid my respects to the Rev. Mr. [James] Blair, the Commissary of Virginia, and by far the most worthy clergyman I have yet met with in all America. He received me with joy, asked me to preach, and wished my stay was to be longer. He has been chiefly instrumental in raising a beautiful college at Williamsburgh, in which is a foundation for about eight scholars, a president, two masters, and professors in the several sciences. Here the gentlemen of Virginia send their children, and as far as I could learn by enquiry, they are under about the same regulation and discipline as in our Universities at home. The present masters came from Oxford. Two of them, I find, were my contemporaries there. I rejoiced in seeing such a place in America. It may be of excellent use, if learning Christ be made one end of their studies, and arts and sciences only introduced and pursued as subservient to that. For want of this, most of our English schools and Universities have sunk into mere seminaries of paganism. Young men's heads are stuffed with heathen mythology, and Christ or Christianity is scarcely so much as named amongst them; so that when they come to be converted, they are obliged to undo what they have been doing for many years. Revive, O Lord, a primitive spirit, and then we may hope for some primitive schools to be erected and encouraged amongst us.

Sunday, Dec. 16. Preached in the morning. Several gentlemen came from York, fourteen miles off, to hear me, and were desirous of my going back to preach at their town, on the morrow. A large audience, I found, might have been expected, could timely notice have been given; but being in great haste, and there being no sermon customarily in the afternoon, I dined with the Commissary, and left Williamsburgh in the afternoon, promising, if possible, to visit these parts again some time in the summer.

Appendix B

Methodists against Slavery in Virginia, 1784; Petition from Frederick County

That your Petitioners are clearly and fully persuaded that Liberty is the Birthright of Mankind, the right of every rational Creature without exception, who has not forfeited that right to the laws of his Country. That the Body of Negroes in this State have been robbed of that right without any such Forfeiture, and therefore ought in Justice to have their rights restored. That the Glorious and ever Memorable Revolution can be Justified on no other principles but what do plead with greater force for the Emancipation of our Slaves. . . . That the Argument, "they were Prisoners of War, when they were Originally purchased" is entirely invalid, for no right of Conquest can justly subject any Man to perpetual Slavery, much less his posterity. . . . That the Argument drawn from the difference of Hair, Features, and Colour, are so beneath the Man of Sense, much more the Christian, that we would not insult the Honourable Assembly by enlarging upon them. . . . But above all, that the deep Debasement of Spirit which is the necessary Consequence of Slavery, incapacitates the human mind (except in a few instances) for the Reception of the Noble and enlarged principles of the Gospel; and therefore to encourage or allow of it, we apprehend to be most opposite to that Catholic [i.e., universal] Spirit of Christianity, which desires the Establishment of the Kingdom of Christ over all the World. . . . And therefore that we humbly entreat the Honourable Assembly as their Superior Wisdom may dictate to them, to pursue the most Prudential, but effectual Method for the immediate or Gradual Extirpation of Slavery. . . .

Further Reading

Catherine L. Albanese, *Sons of the Fathers: The Civil Religion of the American Revolution* (Philadelphia, 1976). Looks at religion not through a denominational framework, but in terms of the broad cultural impact of religion in the Revolutionary age.

Patricia U. Bonomi, *Under the Cope of Heaven: Religion, Society, and Politics in Colonial America* (New York, 1986). The best overview of religion in the colonial period.

Carl Bridenbaugh, *Mitre and Sceptre: Transatlantic Faiths, Ideas, Personalities, and Politics, 1689–1775* (New York, 1962). Reveals the depth of hostility to and anxiety about the possibility of an Anglican bishop's being installed in the colonies.

Thomas E. Buckley, *Church and State in Revolutionary Virginia, 1776–1787* (Charlottesville, Va., 1977). A detailed and well-informed account of Virginia's critical steps toward religious freedom.

Edwin S. Gaustad, *Neither King Nor Prelate: Religion and the New Nation, 1776–1826* (Grand Rapids, Mich., 1993). Compares the popular religion of the churches with the religious thought of such influential Virginians as Washington, Jefferson, and Madison.

Wesley M. Gewehr, *The Great Awakening in Virginia, 1740–1790* (Durham, N. C., 1930). Though an older account, this work is still a valuable guide to the personalities and events of the evangelical revival.

Rhys Isaac, *The Transformation of Virginia, 1740–1790* (Chapel Hill, N. C., 1982). Though covering the same period as Gewehr's volume, this study represents a newer and more inclusive kind of history.

Donald G. Mathews, *Religion in the Old South* (Chicago, 1977). The most sensitive treatment of the rise of the evangelical community (Baptists, Methodists, Presbyterians), with excellent attention to African-American ecclesiastical communities.

William Lee Miller, *The First Liberty: Religion and the American Republic* (New York, 1986). An engagingly written account of the events leading up to the adoption of the First Amendment, a development in which Virginia played a critical role.

Merrill D. Peterson, ed., *Thomas Jefferson: A Reference Biography* (New York, 1986). A topical treatment of the many facets of this celebrated Virginian.
Merrill D. Peterson and Robert C. Vaughan, eds., *The Virginia Statute for Religious Freedom: Its Evolution and Consequences in American History* (New York, 1988). A remarkably detailed account of the collaboration between Jefferson and Madison that made this statute a reality in 1786.
Russell E. Richey, *Early American Methodism* (Bloomington and Indianapolis, Ind., 1991). A valuable new interpretation of the rise and spread of Methodism along the Atlantic coast.
Leigh Eric Schmidt, *Holy Fairs: Scottish Communions and American Revivals in the Early Modern Period* (Princeton, N. J., 1989). A convincing demonstration of the role of sacramentalism in American revivalism, especially among the Presbyterians.
John E. Selby, *The Revolution in Virginia, 1775–1783* (Williamsburg, Va., 1988). A sophisticated interpretation of the pivotal position of the largest colony during the time of the American Revolution.
Harry S. Stout, *The Divine Dramatist: George Whitefield and the Rise of Modern Evangelicalism* (Grand Rapids, Mich., 1991). Highly readable and vitally important for an understanding of the pervasive influence of the Great Awakening's most powerful preacher.
Dell Upton, *Holy Things and Profane: Anglican Parish Churches in Colonial Virginia* (New York, 1986). An architectural study of Virginia's colonial Anglican churches that brings much more to the story than just mortar and bricks.
Gordon S. Wood, *The Creation of the American Republic, 1776–1787* (Chapel Hill, N. C., 1969). A magisterial treatment of all the colonies as they moved into new nationhood.
———, *The Radicalism of the American Revolution* (New York, 1992). A prize-winning interpretive and authoritative history of the American Revolution.
John Frederick Woolverton, *Colonial Anglicanism in North America* (Detroit, Mich., 1984). Given the importance of this denomination in the seventeenth and eighteenth centuries, a survey such as this was way overdue.